D0053893

Civic Center

A Pocket Dictionary of

AZTEC AND MAYAN GODS AND GODDESSES

Clara Bezanilla

The J. Paul Getty Museum · Los Angeles

© 2006 The Trustees of The British Museum

First published in the United Kingdom in 2006
by The British Museum Press
A Divison of The British Museum Company Ltd
38 Russell Square, London WC1B 3QQ

First published in the United States of America
in 2010 by
The J. Paul Getty Museum, Los Angeles

Getty Publications
1200 Getty Center Drive, Suite 500
Los Angeles, California 90049-1682
www.getty.edu

Printed and bound by Tien Wah Press in
Singapore (WT#34620)
First printing by the J. Paul Getty Museum
(12481)

ISBN: 978-1-60606-008-7

Designed and typeset by Peter Bailey
for Proof Books.

CONTENTS

A–Z List of
Gods & Goddesses 4
Guide to the Names 5

THE AZTEC PANTHEON 6

CREATOR GODS

Ometeotl 7

Tezcatlipoca 8

Quetzalcoatl 9

Ehecatl 10–11

GODS OF WAR

Huitzilopochtli 12–13

Tonatiuh 14–15

GODS & GODDESSES OF DEATH

Mictlantecuhtli 16–17

Cihuateteotl 18

GODS & GODDESSES OF LIFE & FERTILITY

Tlaltecuhtli 19

Tlaloc 20–21

Chalchiuhtlicue 22–23

Xipe Totec 24

Xiuhtecuhtli 25

Xochipilli 26–27

Xochiquetzal 28

Chicomecoatl 29

THE MAYA PANTHEON 30

CREATOR GOD

Itzamna (God D) 31

GODS OF DEATH & THE UNDERWORLD

Death God (God A) 32

God Q 33

Smoking God (God L) 34

GODS & GODDESSES OF LIFE & FERTILITY

Sun God (God G) 35

Chac (God B) 36–37

The Moon Goddess (Goddess I) 38–39

Ix Chel (Goddess O) 40

Pauahtun (God N) 41

Maize God (God E) 42–43

OTHER GODS & MYTHS

The Hero Twins 44–45

Ek Chuah (God M) 46

K'awil (God K) 47

Flood Scene 48

A–Z List of Gods & Goddesses

Chac	36–37	Ek Chuah	46	Moon Goddess	38–39
Chalchiuhtlicue	22–23	Hero Twins	44–45	Ometeotl	7
Chicomecoatl	29	Huitzilopochtli	12–13	Pauahtun	41
Cihuateteotl	18	Itzamna	31	God Q	33
Death God	32	Ix Chel	40	Quetzalcoatl	9
Ehecatl	10–11	K'awil	47	Smoking God	34
		Maize God	42–43	Sun God	35
		Mictlantecuhtli	16–17	Tezcatlipoca	8
				Tlaloc	20–21
				Tlaltecuhtli	19
				Tonatiuh	14–15
				Xipe Totec	24
				Xiuhtecuhtli	25
				Xochipilli	26–27
				Xochiquetzal	28

Guide to the Names

Some of the names of the gods and goddesses can be quite tricky to say out loud. The list below shows you how to pronounce the names of gods and goddesses that you will find in this book.

Chac	chak
Chalchiuhtlicue	chal-choo-TLEE-qwae
Chicomecoatl	chi-ko-may-KO-attle
Cihuateteotl	thee-wa-te-TE-ottle
Ehecatl	e-HE-cattle
Ek Chuah	ek choo-ah
Huitzilopochtli	weet-see-lo-POCH-tlee
Itzamna	its-am-NA
Ix Chel	ish chel
K'awil	ka-WEEL
Mictlantecuhtli	mic-tlan-te-KU-tlee
Ometeotl	o-may-TE-ottle
Pauahtun	pa-wah-TOON
Quetzalcoatl	kay-tsal-CO-attle
Tezcatlipoca	teth-ka-tlee-Po-ka
Tlaltecuhtli	tlal-te-KOO-tlee
Tlaloc	TLA-lok
Tonatiuh	toe-NA-chew
Xipe Totec	SHE-pay TOW-tek
Xiuhtecuhtli	shoo-tay-KOO-tlee
Xochipilli	sho-chee-PEE-lee
Xochiquetzal	sho-chee-kay-TSAL

The Aztec Pantheon

For the Aztecs, contrary terms such as life and death were part of the same concept. Their gods often reflect these dual aspects in their character. They can be benevolent and give life but can also destroy life or punish.

According to Aztec myths there were different worlds, also called suns, named by the day in which they ended. Each world or sun was presided over by a different deity.

The cult of different gods and their characteristics varied from region to region

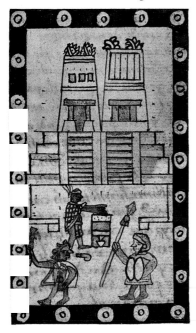

and also through time, as the Aztec empire expanded. Some of the gods have their origin in ancient civilizations that inhabited Mesoamerica (present-day Mexico, Guatemala, Belize and part of Honduras and El Salvador) before the Aztecs. Most deities were patrons of ethnic groups, and activities.

We know about the gods through the codices (screenfold books), early colonial sources (sixteenth- and seventeenth-century documents), and their representation in ceramics, stone sculpture and carvings in wood, bone and jade.

The Great Temple of Tenochtitlan, the Aztec capital, was dedicated to Tlaloc (blue) and Huitzilopochtli (red).

Ometeotl

Ometeotl is the God of Duality. It means that the Aztecs thought the god was both a male and a female, the ancient ancestors of the gods.

The name of this god means 'Two God' and his dual aspect is represented by a couple known by different names, Ometecuhtli and Omecihuatl or Tonacatecuhtli and Tonacacihuatl.

Always portrayed as an aged couple, they are the source of all things, including gods and humans. Quetzalcoatl and Tezcatlipoca, two of their offspring, play a prominent role in the Aztec myths of creation.

Ometeotl, the ancient couple, perform a ceremony surrounded by symbols (glyphs) representing days in the Aztec calendar.

The Aztec universe had thirteen levels above the earth and nine levels below in the Underworld. The thirteenth heaven (the upper-most level) was a place called Omeyocan, the Place of Duality, where Ometeotl resides.

Many prayers were addressed to the couple although no temples are known to be dedicated to this god.

Tezcatlipoca

Tezcatlipoca is one of the creator gods. He is also a god of war and conflict, associated with rulers and sorcerers.

Tezcatlipoca and Quetzalcoatl feature prominently in many of the Aztec myths of creation, of which there are several versions. These gods are sometimes rivals and sometimes allies. Unlike Quetzalcoatl, who is portrayed as a benevolent god who stands for harmony and life, Tezcatlipoca is a god who creates conflict.

Tezcatlipoca presides over the world called the 'First Sun'. The Aztecs called it *Nahui Ocelotl*, which means 'Four Jaguar'. It was inhabited by a race of giants who were devoured by jaguars.

His name in Nahuatl, the Aztec language, means 'Smoking Mirror'. In the codices (screenfold books) he is portrayed with a mirror replacing his foot. Mirrors were used in magic and divination. His body is painted black and his face with black and yellow bands. He often carries the accessories of a warrior: a spear-thrower (*atlatl*), arrows and a shield.

Mosaic mask of Tezcatlipoca. Masks were often worn by priests or idols taking the role of gods for some ceremonies.

Quetzalcoatl

Quetzalcoatl is one of the most important gods in the Aztec pantheon. He is a creator god and the patron of merchants, crafts and knowledge. He is associated with rulers and priests.

Quetzalcoatl, the Feathered Serpent, is a very complex god, with many aspects and spheres of influence. His name, which means 'Quetzal Serpent' in Nahuatl (the language spoken by the Aztecs) has many associations and has created much confusion. It is used for a god worshipped by ancient cultures that preceded the Aztecs. It is also the name of a legendary priest–ruler from Tula, and a title for priests and rulers.

According to an Aztec myth of creation there were four suns (or worlds) before the present one. Each sun was created and destroyed in a different way, and inhabited by a different race of people. Each sun was also presided over by a different deity.

A stone bust representing Quetzalcoatl. His face comes out of the serpent's coils covered in feathers. He wears his characteristic curved shell earrings.

After the destruction of the Fourth Sun, Quetzalcoatl and Tezcatlipoca created the earth and the heavens by tearing apart the earth monster, Tlaltecuhtli.

Ehecatl

Ehecatl is the God of Wind, another aspect of the god Quetzalcoatl.

Ehecatl-Quetzalcoatl presided over the Second Sun. The Aztecs called it *Nahui Ehecatl*, which means 'Four Wind'. This world was destroyed by fierce winds and its people turned into monkeys.

He also created the race of humans that inhabit the Fifth Sun. After floods destroyed the Fourth Sun, the gods created the present world. Ehecatl-Quetzalcoatl went down to the lower level of the Underworld,

This miniature temple is dedicated to Ehecatl. He is wearing his distinctive beaked mask, conical hat and shell pectoral.

where he managed to trick Mictlantecuhtli, the God of Death, and took back the bones of the people of the Fourth Sun. He mixed these bones with some of his blood and gave life to the humans who inhabit the Fifth Sun or present world.

He is also a god associated with agriculture because he brings the rain clouds at the end of the dry season.

Ehecatl is represented in Aztec art with a beak-like mask and wearing curved shell ear ornaments and a pectoral made of a cut conch shell. Temples dedicated to him were round with a conical roof.

A stone figure representing Ehecatl with his beaked mask. He produced the wind by blowing through the mask. The Wind God swept the paths to clear the way for the arrival of the Rain God, Tlaloc.

Huitzilopochtli

Huitzilopochtli is the patron god of the Aztecs. He is a god of war and a manifestation of the sun.

Huitzilopochtli told his people to settle in a place where they found an eagle perched on a cactus and eating a snake. Tenochtitlan, the Aztec capital, was built on an island in an ancient lake.

Huitzilopochtli was a tribal god who, according to Aztec legends about migration, led his people to the Valley of Mexico and indicated the place where they should settle. His name in Nahuatl, the Aztec language, means 'Humming Bird'.

His mother was the old Earth Goddess, Coatlicue. Huitzilopochtli was born in full warrior costume and armed with his weapon, the Xiuhcoatl (Fire Serpent). He slaughtered his sister Coyolxauhqui, the moon goddess, and his brothers, the stars, who were attempting to kill their mother, ashamed by her pregnancy. The myth of his birth was re-enacted through human sacrifice and blood offerings to ensure the sun's daily victory.

His cult was more important at Tenochtitlan, the Aztec capital, where one of the two sanctuaries of the Great Temple was dedicated to him. Very few representations of this god are known in Aztec art.

The Xiuhcoatl or Fire Serpent was Huitzilopochtli's war weapon. It was used to kill his brothers and sister. He also sometimes wears it as a back ornament, as does Xiuhtecuhtli, the Fire God.

Tonatiuh

Tonatiuh is the Sun God and warriors were dedicated to serving him.

Tonatiuh presided over the Fifth Sun, called *Nahui Ollin* by the Aztecs, which means 'Four Movement'. This world will be destroyed by earthquakes and its people devoured by sky monsters.

According to an Aztec creation myth, the gods sacrificed themselves at Teotihuacan, a mythical ancient city, to create a new sun. Two of them threw themselves into a fire and became the sun and the moon. The sun demanded the blood of the other gods who, with their sacrifice, set in motion the Fifth Sun. And so, humans had to offer blood, just as the gods did, in

This stone pendant shows Tonatiuh surrounded by a sun disc and wearing a headdress made of eagle feathers. Eagles were associated with the sun and warfare.

order to keep the sun moving across the sky.

Warriors were in charge of providing the Sun God with sacrificial victims. Those who died in battle escorted the sun through the journey from dawn to noon.

Tonatiuh is usually depicted with a solar disk and a headdress made of eagle feathers.

This is a *cuauhxicalli* or 'eagle vessel', used for the hearts of sacrificial victims. The symbol inside the solar disc is Four Movement, the name of one of the days in the Aztec ritual calendar.

Mictlantecuhtli

Mictlantecuhtli is the God of Death. He is the Lord of the Underworld, a place called Mictlan, where he lived with his counterpart Mictlancihuatl.

Each of the Underworld's levels was presided over by a different god associated with death. The deceased went to a particular level in Mictlan according to the circumstances of their death. The ninth level, where Mictlantecuhtli resided, was the place where the 'souls' of those who died of natural causes went. To reach this level, they had to negotiate all sorts of obstacles. The dead were cremated with

A stone carving of Mictlantecuhtli shows his skeletal face with large ear ornaments and a headdress. The Death God lived in the last level of Mictlan, the Underworld.

some of their possessions, especially the tools they used in life, to help them through their dangerous journey.

Mictlantecuhtli was the guardian of the bones of the dead. He was associated with nocturnal birds, such as the owl. Owls were associated with shamans and were the Death God's messengers. They were considered to be a bad omen: their presence and nocturnal calls were believed to announce death or misfortune.

Owls, the messengers of the Death God, are not often represented in Aztec art. This sculpture was probably used as a ceremonial vessel.

Cihuateteotl

Cihuateteotl is the spirit or soul of a woman who has died during childbirth.

Representations of Cihuateteotl are fairly common in Aztec art. She is shown with a skeletal face and dressed in a skirt tied around her waist with a belt made of serpents. Many of the stone sculptures have come from Tenochtitlan, the Aztec capital.

Stone sculptures of Cihuateteotl display dates of the sacred Aztec calendar on the top of her head. It was believed that the Cihuateteo descended to earth on those days and tried to kidnap young children.

Cihuateteotl was considered an equal of the warrior who escorted the sun from the east to its maximum point at midday. Like the dead warrior, Cihuateteotl accompanied the sun in its journey across the sky, but on its descent to the west, where these spirits lived.

A stone sculpture of Cihuateteotl. The sign '1 Monkey', one of the days in the ritual Aztec calendar, is carved on her head.

Tlaltecuhtli

Tlaltecuhtli is an earth goddess, associated with death and regeneration, and birth.

Although her name means 'Earth Lord' she is always depicted as a female. She is also referred to as the 'Earth Monster'.

Tlaltecuhtli was torn apart by the creator gods, Tezcatlipoca and Quetzalcoatl, to create the heavens and earth. These gods transformed themselves into two large serpents and grabbed hold of a foot and hand each, tearing the monster apart. The other gods tried to appease her and made flowers, grass, trees and all plants needed by humans, grow from her body. Out of her body also came the mountains, valleys, caves and rivers.

The image of Tlaltecuhtli is usually carved at the bottom of Aztec monuments and sculptures. She is shown in a squatting position, with her arms raised, clutching skulls, and her head looking upwards. Symbols associated with death, such as skulls and cross bones, adorn her body. She was invoked by midwives during difficult child labour.

A drawing of Tlaltecuhtli shows her squatting with her head and arms extended upwards. Cross bones and skulls decorate her body.

Tlaloc

Tlaloc is the God of Rain and Lightning, and the patron of agriculture.

Tlaloc was an important god in the Aztec pantheon. His role in agriculture was vital because he ensured that rain arrived on time after the dry season. But he could also provoke floods and storms.

He is an ancient god, worshipped by other Mesoamerican cultures for hundreds of years before the arrival of the Aztecs. At Tenochtitlan, the Aztec capital, one of the twin shrines in the Great Temple was dedicated to Tlaloc. He is usually portrayed with goggled eyes and fangs coming out of his mouth.

His feminine counterpart is Chalchiuhtlicue, associated with ground water and the sea.

Mixtec artisans were much appreciated for their skills at Tenochtitlan where many of them lived. This small head, representing the Rain God, is carved in Mixtec style.

The Tlaloque, his attendants, were each associated with a mountain. Mountains were considered to be sacred places. Ceremonies dedicated to the rain gods took place at various hill sites in the Valley of Mexico. Aztec rulers made pilgrimages and brought offerings to images of rain gods set up on Mount Tlaloc, in the Valley of Mexico.

The image of Tlaloc, the Aztec Rain God, is carved on a side of this stone box. Water and ears of corn flow from the vessel he holds.

Chalchiuhtlicue

Chalchiuhtlicue is a water goddess, associated with springs, rivers and lakes, and also with birth.

According to an Aztec creation myth, Chalchiuhtlicue presided over the Fourth Sun. The Aztecs called this world *Nahui Atl*, which means 'Four Water'. It was destroyed by floods and its people turned into fish.

Her name in Nahuatl means 'She of the Jade Skirt'. As a water goddess, she was associated with birth. Newborn children were dedicated to her because water was believed to purify. Like Tlaloc, she is also related to the earth and fertility.

Chalchiuhtlicue is wearing a *quechquemitl*, a shawl fringed with a row of tassels. This type of shawl is still worn by women in some areas of Mexico today.

Figures made of organic material (resin and copal) representing Chalchiuhtlicue and the Rain God Tlaloc have been found in a cave to the east of Mexico City. But the larger number of known representations of this goddess are stone sculptures. She is usually represented as a young woman with her hair arranged in two large tassels on both sides of the head, and wearing the traditional shawl (*quechquemitl*) over a long skirt. In the codices she appears coloured in blue.

Chalchiuhtlicue's headdress is complemented by a bow made of pleated bark paper, usually worn by fertility deities. The same bow can be seen on a sculpture of Xiuhtecuhtli, the God of Fire (see page 25).

Xipe Totec

Xipe Totec is a god of fertility and patron of goldsmiths. He was one of the four children of the couple Ometecuhtli and Omecihuatl, from whom the gods originated.

Xipe Totec is a fertility god who was worshipped by other ancient Mexican civilizations, like many other Aztec gods. His name in Nahuatl means 'Our Lord the Flayed One'.

He is usually represented as a figure wearing a human skin on his face and body, which seems to symbolize the new spring growth. He represents the regeneration of life through death.

During the springtime festivities, which were held in his honour, war captives were dedicated to him. The victims were tied to a round stone and killed by four warriors. The corpses were flayed and the skin worn by their captors for twenty days.

Xipe Totec was also the patron of goldsmiths. During their festivals, they adorned an impersonator of the god with feathers and gold, and made rich offerings at Xipe Totec's temple in the Aztec capital.

These masks are intended to represent Xipe Totec. Representations of this god show him, or a priest, wearing the skin of flayed victims.

Xiuhtecuhtli

Xiuhtecuhtli is the God of Fire, also identified with the Old God, Huehueteotl, with whom he shares many attributes.

Xiuhtecuhtli was associated with rulers and warriors and presided over time and the calendar. He played a prominent role in the New Fire ceremonies, celebrated every fifty-two years, an important cycle for the Aztecs.

His name means the 'Turquoise Lord'. In the codices, Xiuhtecuhtli's face is painted with black and red pigment. He carries the Xiuhcoatl, the Fire Serpent, as a back ornament, and a turquoise pectoral in the form of a butterfly. In stone sculpture his image is rendered in the nude, except for a loincloth, and with two teeth protruding from the corners of his mouth, a characteristic of the Old God, Huehueteotl. But, unlike Huehueteotl, he is always portrayed as a young man.

Xiuhtecuhtli is wearing a bark headdress and a loincloth. The circles on his headband are symbols for fire.

The cult of the Fire God went back many centuries before Aztec times and extended throughout Mesoamerica.

Xochipilli

Xochipilli is a fertility god, associated with flowers and plants. He is also a patron of music and dance.

Xochipilli was associated with maize, as well as flowers. His name in Nahuatl means 'Flower Prince'.

He is the patron of music, dancing and games. Music and dance played an important role in Aztec religious and public ceremonies. Religious festivals dedicated to a particular god were celebrated each month (of twenty days). A variety of instruments were used to

Xochipilli, the Flower Prince, is a god of fertility. Celebrations in his honour took place in June, at the beginning of the growing season when the rains had arrived.

accompany these festivities such as flutes, drums (including the *teponaztli*) and conch shells. Archaeologists have found miniature instruments buried with images of Xochipilli.

His cult was most important in places such as Xochimilco (in the south of present-day Mexico City) where flowers and plants were grown on raised fields called *chinampas*, and still are today.

Xochipilli, like most Aztec gods, had another aspect to him. He could strike down with terrible diseases those who did not observe the sacred fasting days.

This wooden drum called ***teponaztli*** was played by striking the two tongues on top with drumsticks. It was hollowed-out and carved from a piece of hardwood.

Xochiquetzal

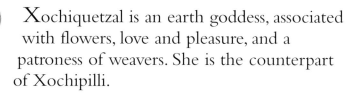

Xochiquetzal is an earth goddess, associated with flowers, love and pleasure, and a patroness of weavers. She is the counterpart of Xochipilli.

She was also associated with childbirth, like other fertility and earth goddesses. She would look after pregnant women and young mothers.

Xochiquetzal was a patroness of weaving and other arts practised by women of the Aztec nobility and by specialist artisans, such as painters, featherworkers and metalsmiths. During the festivals celebrated in her honour the Aztecs would dance dressed up in costumes representing jaguars, monkeys and other animals.

Her name in Nahuatl means 'Flower Quetzal'. She was portrayed as a beautiful young woman, richly dressed and wearing gold jewellery. She often wears a headdress made of two tufts of quetzal feathers.

Many small clay figurines have been found representing Xochiquetzal and other fertility goddesses. They were made in moulds and were mass produced for use in household worship as opposed to state religion.

A small clay figurine representing the goddess Xochiquetzal.

Chicomecoatl

Chicomecoatl is a fertility goddess, related especially to maize, the most important crop for the Aztecs.

She is a goddess of food plants and is usually represented carrying ears of corn in her hands. Her large headdress is rectangular and decorated with rosettes. This headdress, called *amacalli* (house of paper) was made of rigid bark paper and worn during the festivals by the impersonator of the goddess.

Festivities in her honour were celebrated during the fourth Aztec month, just before the beginning of the rainy season when maize is planted. During these ceremonies, people decorated the altars in their households with maize plants while corn seeds were blessed in the temples.

Chicomecoatl's name means 'Seven Serpent', a date in the Aztec calendar. Gods and goddesses, humans, and even the different worlds were often named after one of these dates.

A stone sculpture showing Chicomecoatl wearing her headdress made of rigid bark paper.

The Maya Pantheon

The ancient Maya people occupied a large territory that includes modern Mexico, Guatemala, Belize, Honduras and El Salvador. Their cultural history and languages were diverse. Their pantheon consisted of a large number of deities. Some of their gods were shared with other Mesoamerican peoples while others were gods from other cultures added to the Maya pantheon.

Maya gods often shared the same characteristics and spheres of influence, which sometimes changed through time, mainly from the Classic period (*c.* AD 250–900) to the Postclassic period (*c.* AD 900–1530). Their characteristics also varied from region to region. However, many of the gods featuring in Classic sources can be recognized during the Postclassic period.

The main sources of information for Maya gods are the codices, early colonial sources (sixteenth- and seventeenth-century documents), ceramics and mural paintings. During the nineteenth century, a scholar called Paul Schellhas studied the gods in the three known codices. Maya hieroglyphs could not be read at the time and he named the gods with a letter of the Roman alphabet, a system that is still in use today.

A drawing from a Maya codex showing some of the gods in the Maya pantheon.

Itzamna (God D)

Itzamna is one of the most important Maya gods. He is a creator god, associated with writing and divination.

Itzamna is Lord of the Heavens and Earth, associated with creation and birth. He was credited with the invention of writing and 'books', and is often portrayed painting or as a scribe. His counterpart is the old goddess Ix Chel.

Also known as God D, he is always represented as an old man, with a large square eye and a hooked nose. He shares some attributes with the Sun God. In the codices he appears repeatedly with the Maize God or seated on a throne, facing other deities, such as God N or God L.

The sign *Akbal* (meaning night and darkness) usually appears on his headdress. This sign represents a mirror, a device used in divination. Itzamna was a wise god, with esoteric knowledge, and he was believed to have the power of healing. He was therefore invoked as a god of medicine.

Itzamna is a creator god. He is a wise deity who rules over the heavens and other Maya gods.

Death God (God A)

Kimi, the God of Death, is the Lord of the Maya Underworld. He is associated with death, war and sacrifice.

Also known as God A, he is portrayed totally or partially as a skeleton – often shown with black spots that represent the decay of the flesh. His aspect is sometimes terrifying, appearing in scenes related to executions. At other times, he is shown as a grotesque and laughable figure, with an enormous belly.

Kimi, the Death God, lives in the lowest of the nine levels of the Underworld. His companions are the owl and other creatures related to death and evil omens.

The Death God holding an offering. The black spots on his body represent decaying flesh. Sometimes his ribs are also showing.

The ancient Maya thought that people who had a violent death went directly to one of the thirteen heavens. Everyone else went to the Underworld, where the God of Death dictated their fate. The modern Maya from Yucatan (Mexico) still believe today that he creeps around the houses of sick people, waiting for a future victim.

God Q

God Q is associated with violent death and sacrifice.

He can be recognized by a black band that runs around his eyes and down his cheek. This band appears as either a solid or dotted line. Dotted lines can often be seen on his body as well.

Many of his symbols are associated with sacrifice and death, such as death eyes, a death collar and a knotted headdress made of paper or cloth.

God Q is frequently shown with Kimi, the God of Death, and holding stone weapons. He is also often portrayed with the Rain God Chac in execution scenes.

In other scenes, he appears attacking Ek Chuah, a god of merchants, with a spear. This has been interpreted as a representation of the dangerous journeys that merchants embarked upon.

God Q is also related to war and he is shown in the codices burning and destroying buildings with a torch and spear.

God Q holds an offering of cacao. Cacao was much appreciated by the ancient Maya. Cacao beans became a form of currency.

Smoking God (God L)

God L is one of the principal gods of the Underworld. He is associated with rain and lightning and he is a patron of merchants.

Most representations of this god appear during the Classic period, always as an aged man. He can be recognized by his large square eye and he has jaguar markings on his body. His headdress represents the Moan bird (an owl) associated with the Underworld; sometimes only the feathers of this bird are shown. He often appears smoking a cigar, hence his nickname 'Smoking God'.

Although he is associated with the Underworld he also has attributes related to life-giving rain and agricultural fertility. In the codices he is often painted black. Modern Maya use black soot from copal smoke for ceremonies related to rain.

God L is a patron of merchants for the Maya of the Classic period. He is often represented carrying bundles, sometimes showing precious goods, such as quetzal feathers.

The Smoking God, a god of the Underworld, with black markings on his face and body. The Moan bird is part of his headdress.

Sun God (God G)

K'inich Ajaw, the Sun God, is an important god in the Maya pantheon. He is associated with rulership and dynastic descent.

The first part of his name, K'inich (meaning sun-face), was used as an important title for Maya lords.

Known also as God G, he can be recognized by the sign *kin* (sun) which usually appears on his face or body. Like Itzamna and other old gods, he has a prominent nose and square eyes. Two large teeth and curls come out of his mouth. In the Postclassic period he is often represented wearing a beard. In certain Maya areas the rays of the sun are referred to as 'the beard of the sun'.

A stone sculpture from the Maya city of Copan representing the Sun God. His large square eyes and protruding teeth are clearly visible.

Sometimes the Sun God has jaguar markings on his face. Jaguars were associated with night and the Underworld. The Sun was believed to go through the Underworld before it rose again in the morning.

The Sun God was also connected with war and sacrifice, especially by decapitation.

Chac (God B)

Chac, the Rain God, is one of the oldest and most important deities of the Maya, even today. He is in charge of rain, lightning and water.

A page of a codex showing Chac, the Rain God (first and third figures from left), on the open jaws of serpents.

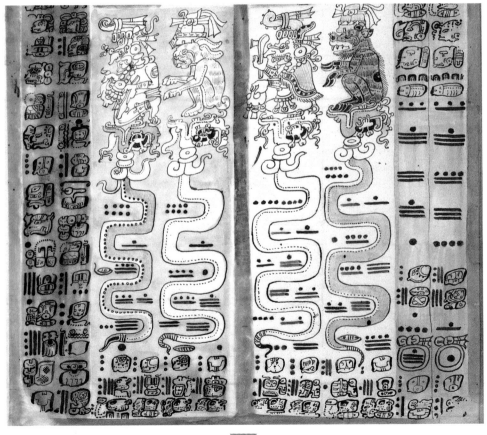

Also known as God B, he can be easily recognized by his facial features and headdress. He has a long, hanging nose and two spirals curling out of his mouth. He often carries stone axes and serpents, both associated with lightning.

Chac is a patron of agriculture, often portrayed in *cenotes* (water holes) or in streams of water. According to a Maya myth, he provided the first maize plant, a vital crop for the Maya, by cracking open a rock with lightning.

He is also associated with war, using his lightning axes as weapons, together with a shield. In the Postclassic period, he was also related to sacrifice.

He is the god most often represented in the codices, engaged in a wide range of activities with other gods.

Chac holding a shield and a serpent in his right hand and a stone axe in his left.

The Moon Goddess (Goddess I)

Goddess I is the Moon Goddess. She is usually represented as a young and beautiful woman, with the moon crescent and a rabbit.

Like the Aztecs, the Maya saw the shape of a rabbit on the patterns that are especially visible on the full moon.

The moon and the sun were associated with rulership. At Yaxchilan, an important Maya city, the mothers of the kings were represented with moon symbols, and their fathers with sun symbols.

The moon was associated with female aspects, as is the case in many other cultures around the world. The Moon Goddess presided over pregnancy, childbirth and weaving. The Maya of Yucatan still believe today that pregnant women are in danger during a lunar eclipse. The ancient Maya thought that lunar eclipses, when the moon disappears totally or partially, were evil omens. Several pages of one of the codices are dedicated to descriptions of solar and lunar eclipses.

The Moon Goddess carrying the Rain God Chac on her back. She is often shown with a rabbit and a moon crescent.

A page from a codex describing an eclipse. The Moon Goddess is shown with a rope around her neck. Her closed eye and the dark spot on her cheek indicate that she is dead.

Ix Chel (Goddess O)

Ix Chel is an old and powerful goddess, associated with creative as well as destructive forces. She is the counterpart of the creator god Itzamna.

She is always portrayed as an old goddess, usually painted in red in the codices, often depicted as a frightening being with claws and fangs. She wears a twisted serpent as a headdress and her skirt is frequently decorated with symbols relating to death such as crossed bones.

Ix Chel was associated with floods and storms. Her serpent headdress may be connected to this, since serpents were widely associated with water and lightning. She is often shown in the codices pouring water from inverted pots. She also appears in a scene which is believed to represent the floods that destroyed the world. This is a myth shared with other Mesoamerican people, including the Aztecs.

Ix Chel is also associated with creative forces and was considered to be the goddess of childbirth, medicine, divination and weaving.

The old goddess Ix Chel with a twisted serpent as a headdress. She is pouring water from a vessel.

Pauahtun (God N)

Pauahtun is an important god in the Maya pantheon. He is associated with thunder, music and drunkenness.

Known as God N, he is often portrayed with a tortoise carapace or a conch shell. Tortoise and conch shells were used as musical instruments and to reproduce the sound of thunder. Pauahtun was a god of thunder and mountains. He was frequently depicted with Chac, the God of Rain, sometimes holding an axe, which was Chac's lightning weapon.

He is sometimes represented as a sacred mountain holding up the sky. For the Maya, particular gods had the task of supporting the sky. Colonial accounts refer to four skybearers called *bacabs*, who played an important role in New Year ceremonies. These skybearers were another aspect of Pauahtun, who divided himself into four people, corresponding to the four directions of the world.

Pauahtun, the God of Thunder, was often pictured with a conch shell.

Maize God (God E)

The Maize God is associated with abundance and prosperity. He is widely represented in Maya art.

The Maize God, with his delicate facial features and vibrant youth, represents the Maya ideal of beauty. He is usually portrayed with a lavish headdress, representing a stylized ear of corn; his hair is the silk of the cob.

The severed head of the Maize God.

Maize had an important role in Maya creation myths. According to the *Popol Vuh*, a sacred book of the Quiché Maya from the colonial period, gods created humans out of yellow and white corn. Originally, the gods had tried to make humans with clay and wood but their attempts were unsuccessful.

The main characters in this account are the Hero Twins and their father Hun Hunahpu, a maize god. In one episode, Hun Hunahpu and his brother were called by the lords of

Xibalba, the Maya Underworld, because they were disturbed by their constant ball playing. Having failed all the tests given by these lords, they were sacrificed. The Maize God's head was cut off and placed on a tree.

A sculpture of the Maize God. Eight images, including this one, were found in a temple from the ancient Maya city of Copan.

The Hero Twins

The Hero Twins are the main characters in the *Popol Vuh*, a sacred book of the Quiché Maya. It recounts creation myths and the story of the Hero Twins.

Hunahpu and Xbalanque, the Hero Twins, are the children of Hun Hunahpu, the Maize God, and of Xquic, a lady from the Underworld. They are frequently depicted in Maya art and writing from the Classic period, especially on ceramic vessels.

On one occasion, the Lords of Xibalba called the twins to their presence, as they had done to their father and uncle, enraged by their constant ball playing. But the Hero Twins managed to trick the death deities of the Underworld. They killed one of the principal gods and the inhabitants of Xibalba lost their great power.

On another occasion, the Hero Twins killed a monstrous bird, called Vucub Caquix (Seven Macaw), with their blow-guns. After floods destroyed the world inhabited by a race of wooden people, this vicious bird wanted to rule the world.

The Maize God coming out from the earth, represented by a tortoise carapace. The Hero Twins stand on both sides. Hunahpu is shown with black markings on his body and Xbalanque with jaguar ears and beard.

Ek Chuah (God M)

Ek Chuah is the God of Merchants and Travellers in Yucatan during the Postclassic period.

Also known as God M, he can be recognized by his long nose and hanging lower lip that sticks out. Ek means 'black', and in the codices he is usually painted black. He is a strange-looking god, unlike any other Maya deity, and he may be a foreign god added to the Maya pantheon.

While the Smoking God was a god of merchants during the Classic period, Ek Chuah takes these attributes during the Postclassic period. Like the Smoking God, Ek Chuah is associated with Moan, the owl.

As a merchant god he was associated with cacao, and people growing these trees held festivities in his honour. Cacao beans were very valuable for the Maya, who used them as currency.

Long distance merchants had to face great dangers on their travels to foreign lands. Sometimes people embarking on a journey would make offerings to Ek Chuah asking for a safe return.

Ek Chuah was the god of merchants and travellers.

K'awil (God K)

God K is associated with rulership and lightning.

A ruler of the ancient Maya city of Copan, holding an offering plate with the head of God K.

God K's name, like that of many other Maya gods, varies through time and from region to region. In Classic times, his name was K'awil while in Yucatan, in the Postclassic period, he was known as Bolon Dzacab.

He can be recognized by his long upturned nose. During the Classic period he is portrayed with a serpent replacing his foot. An axe blade or a smoking torch comes out of a mirror on his forehead.

He is associated with royal lineages and descent, and he is often depicted on stone carvings and monuments as the 'Manikin Sceptre', a staff carried by rulers. He is usually shown in full figure, although sometimes only the head is portrayed.

He appears frequently with Chac, the God of Rain, as a zoomorphic axe, representing a lightning axe. Sometimes his serpent-foot is shown as a fire serpent, an element associated with lightning and thunderbolts.

Flood Scene

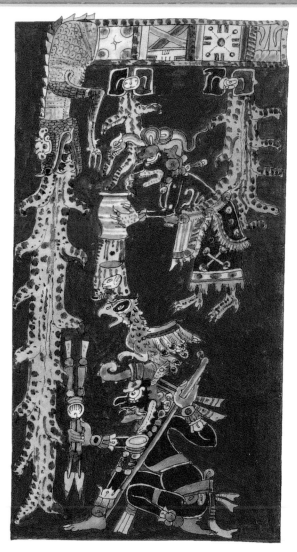

The old goddess Ix Chel in a scene believed to represent a flood. Like the Aztecs, the Maya thought that a flood had once destroyed the world.